ADOLESCENT CO-OCCURRING DISORDERS SERIES

Substance Use and Mood Disorders

Janice Gabe, LCSW, CADAC

HAZELDEN

Hazelden
Center City, Minnesota 55012-0176

1-800-328-9000
1-651-213-4590 (Fax)
www.hazelden.org

About the author

Janice Gabe is the founder and president of New Perspectives of Indiana, Inc., a counseling, consultation, and training corporation based in Indianapolis. She has a master's degree in social work from the University of Illinois at Chicago. Since 1979, she has been working with addicted adolescents with co-occurring disorders and family systems. She began her career working with severely emotionally disturbed adolescents and was involved in developing one of the first adolescent addiction treatment programs in Illinois. She subsequently has held several key clinical and administrative positions in a variety of adult and adolescent programs.

Janice Gabe has served as a consultant to universities, schools, and a variety of inpatient and outpatient adolescent treatment programs. She has authored numerous books, including *A Professional's Guide to Dual Disorders in Adolescence, Cultures of Change: Recovery and Relapse Prevention for Dually Diagnosed and Addicted Adolescents, Making the Grade: The Teen's Guide to Homework Success, Value-Based Parenting,* and *Value-Based Consequences.* In addition, she has produced two sets of parenting videos. She is the featured subject matter expert in the Hazelden video *Adolescents and Co-occurring Disorders.* She has lectured extensively throughout the United States and is widely recognized as one of the country's leading experts in adolescent treatment.

Cover design by David Spohn
Interior design and typesetting by Kinne Design

CONTENTS

FACILITATOR'S INFORMATION

Substance Use and Mood Disorders is a culmination of twenty-two years of experience working with adolescents with mood problems. The terms *mood disorder* and *mood problem* will be used interchangeably in this workbook, although a mood disorder typically refers to a diagnosis and a mood problem does not.

Many adolescents with mood problems also use, abuse, or are addicted to mood-altering substances. The use of substances in this population is often overlooked. Professionals often ask, "Which issue should we address first: the substance use or the mood problem?" The answer is both at the same time. The next question follows shortly thereafter, "How do we do that?" This workbook is the answer to that question.

What Is Covered Here?

Professionals will find a comprehensive, simple, and practical approach to helping teens with mood disorders and substance-abuse problems. This workbook will be helpful for teens with substance-abuse issues experiencing major depression, dysthymia, and depression associated with bipolar mood disorder.

Major depression can disrupt daily activities like going to school, studying, concentrating, sleeping, working, eating, and socializing with others. According to DSM-IV criteria, a major depressive disorder is characterized by one or more major depressive episodes. The criteria for a major depressive episode in adolescents is five (or more) of the following symptoms during the same two-week period representing a change from previous functioning; at least one of the symptoms is either depressed mood or loss of interest or pleasure. Most of these symptoms crop up nearly every day. The symptoms are listed below:

- depressed mood for most of the day linked to feeling sad or empty and being in an irritable mood
- lacking interest in pleasure
- failing to make expected weight gains as a child or significant weight gain; loss of appetite
- insomnia
- psychomotor agitation
- fatigue or loss of energy
- feelings of worthlessness
- diminished ability to think or concentrate or not being able to make decisions
- recurrent thoughts of death, suicidal ideation

See the DSM-IV for more information on specific major depressive episode criteria information.

Dysthymia is a less severe form of depression where people simply don't feel good most of the time. According to DSM-IV diagnostic criteria, dysthymic disorder in adolescents is defined as depressed mood for most of the day, for more days than not, or for at least a year. Dysthymic disorder requires the presence while depressed of two (or more) of the following:

- poor appetite or overeating
- insomnia or hypersomnia
- low energy or fatigue
- low self-esteem
- poor concentration or difficulty making decisions
- feelings of hopelessness

See the DSM-IV for more information on specific mood disorder criteria information.

Consider this workbook a handy tool to use with adolescents struggling with mood and substance-abuse problems. Adolescents typically measure their depression not on their level of functioning but rather on how much emotional pain they feel—mild, moderate, or severe. Prior to using this workbook, it's helpful if you have access or knowledge about the topic of depression in adolescents and basic information about adolescent substance-abuse and drinking patterns. Teens can and will get better when they are given accurate information about their mood, are taught skills to help better understand their mood, are provided with practical and useful knowledge about managing their moods, and begin to see the link between their mood management and substance-abuse problems.

How Is This Workbook Structured?

This flexible workbook can be used with adolescents during one-on-one sessions or in group settings (both open and closed). Implementing a session is simple. Start by briefly introducing a workbook topic, discuss the topic with the adolescent, and then give a homework assignment. Worksheets should eventually be returned to you for your review. Consider this workbook as a clinical tool that can be used to enhance your work with teens.

Who Should Facilitate This Workbook?

Any professional who works in a clinical capacity with teens will find this workbook helpful. Social workers, psychologists, school counselors, youth ministers, addiction counselors, marriage and family therapists, and adolescent/young adult therapists and counselors will find this workbook to be a valuable resource.

Who Is the Client?

The target audience is young people between the ages of twelve and twenty with a mood disorder who use alcohol or any other mood-altering substance. This workbook can also be used with clients who are not using alcohol or other mood-altering substances. In cases like this, assign the material that addresses physical, cognitive, and behavioral dimensions of mood problems covered on pages 7–93.

Any references to substance abuse can be used as a prevention tool. If your client's primary problem is substance abuse and it appears to be creating mood problems, focus first on the parts of the workbook that address substance abuse (pages 95–129). The section on marijuana (pages 113–129) will be particularly helpful if your client is smoking pot. From there, you can assign other parts of the workbook that make the link between mood disorder and substance abuse.

How Can this Workbook Be Used?

This workbook was designed to be flexible. That's why we've chosen the reproducible worksheet format. It can be used in the course of dealing with an adolescent one-on-one or in groups. In individual counseling or therapy, adolescents can work through the workbook section by section. Some adolescents are open and receptive to completing homework assignments outside of a session. These assignments can then be discussed in a subsequent session. Some adolescents do poorly with homework assignments. Noncompliance might have something to do with problems focusing, poor time management, reading difficulty, or simple therapeutic resistance. In this situation, the worksheet assignments can be completed verbally during the session. Some clinical settings such as residential, intensive outpatient, or inpatient treatment provide an opportunity to monitor completion of homework.

This workbook can also be used in conjunction with family or group therapy. The exercises are designed to promote discussion on topics relating to mood management and substance abuse.

How Long Will It Take to Complete this Workbook?

How long it takes to go through the entire workbook depends on the client and the context in which the workbook is being used. Spend more time on the areas that address the adolescent's situation and less on areas that aren't an issue for them. The key is to know your client and be flexible. Teens should be given an adequate amount of time (whatever they need) to complete each assignment.

What Is the Goal of This Workbook?

This workbook is designed as a comprehensive model for treating adolescents with mood problems (depression) and substance-abuse issues. Adolescents will have a better understanding of their mood problems, apply this knowledge to their own mood experiences, and ultimately learn to manage their mood without using mood-altering substances.

◇

WHAT'S IN A MOOD?

WHAT'S IN A MOOD?

Welcome

Hello, my name is Janice. I am a therapist who has worked with teenagers for over twenty years. I know, that makes me sound really old! That's one reason I am so wise. By working with thousands of adolescents, I have learned much about great kids who suffer with mood problems. Along the way, I have discovered a few things to help adolescents who have trouble with depression feel better. I wrote this workbook hoping that more teens who feel bad will learn ways to feel better. I hope it is a helpful tool for you.

• EMILY'S STORY •

Hello, my name is Emily. Maybe to others it is not so strange that I am twenty-two years old and a senior in college, but to me, it is the most amazing thing ever! I spent much of my time in high school struggling with my mood and depression.

Looking back, it seems like a completely different life. In high school, I had to perform two tasks every day. First, try not to kill myself. Second, try not to kill anyone else. Everything else didn't matter too much to me. My friends were always disappointing me and my teachers were not compassionate people. Most of all, I felt like I had the biggest secret and no one could ever know about it because they would not understand it. I remember having what I later found out were panic attacks every day. I would just be sitting in class and all of a sudden, I had to leave. It wasn't anything in particular that made me lose it. It was this sudden wave that would hit me where I wanted to kill or hurt myself or scream at someone. At the very least, I couldn't go on just sitting there and listening to some teacher talk about algebra. I spent more time in my car than the classroom. It was one of the only things I could do to calm myself down. I would leave (yes, I confess I skipped school) and just drive. Then, I would go back to school and attempt to make it though the rest of the day.

While I somehow managed to have boyfriends, go to games and dances, and do the "normal" things that "normal" people do in high school, memories of my hospitalization in the middle of my junior year creep into my mind. Today, I change my mind constantly about what high school meant to me. No matter how good my life gets and how much I accomplish, when someone asks me, "So, how did you like high school?" I still get that gnaw in my stomach and honestly say that I hated it. Even though I'm a senior at Indiana University and doing well today, I am still jealous of people who were prom queens, honor students, or even those who made it through without scars and a hospital record.

On my second day at college, there was not a cloud in the sky. It was warm and everyone was being so nice. After classes, I went on a picnic with some friends. I started feeling like maybe things were going to be instantly better. But they weren't. That same night, I felt horrible. I felt that way every night that first year. But I stuck with it. And eventually, it got better and I felt happier. Looking back at my high school experience, there are a few things I wish I'd have done that I'd like to share with you.

1. **Control what you can.** You have to go to school, that's a fact. To help you stay in school, talk to your teachers and administrators about your problems. Who knows, maybe they can help or refer you to someone who can. At the very least, if they know what you are going through maybe they won't suspend you if you have trouble or miss a few classes.

2. **Control the things that are only going to make you feel worse.** My pet peeve to this day is depressed people who are also using alcohol or nonprescription drugs. Don't do drugs when you are depressed, they will only make you feel worse!

3. **Be honest with yourself and your good friends.** If you are depressed, just admit it. Don't hide it from your friends or they might think you are being distant and rude. When people know about your depression or crazy moods, you may often be asked, "Are you okay?" This can be annoying, but at least if people keep asking, someone will be there when you look at them and say, "No, I'm not."

4. **Ask for help if you need it.** Now this is the one that I still struggle with most. I still get sad and moody a couple of times a year and have problems letting people know how to help me. It can be a double-edged sword because you know you need help, but you don't know how anyone can help. Just try. I let my college roommates know when I am down. They do things like stay with me and watch rented movies when they know I need them to be there—that makes me feel better. I don't feel so alone. No one expects that if you ask them for help that they will solve all your problems. Just think of something small they can do for you and then take the big step of telling them what it is.

I am extremely happy with my life now. I finally have a great group of friends. I am doing really well in college. And most important, I feel like I can do anything. If you asked me in high school what I wanted to be when I grew up, I wouldn't have answered because I sincerely thought I would be dead before that. But now, I have plans and things to look forward to. I don't have it all figured out, but I have discovered that figuring it out is half the fun.

My advice for people who are suffering from depression and trying to be a teenager at the same time is, "Hang in there. It will get better!"

Janice's Comments

Emily is a young lady who had one of the worst mood problems I have ever seen. Keeping her alive from one day to the next sometimes felt like a full-time job. She would often get mad at me and fire me as her therapist once a month or so. One of the greatest days in my life was one New Year's Eve when Emily called to tell me that I had always told her there would be a day when she would be happy that she had kept herself alive. She informed me that, "This is the day!"

Through therapy and medication, Emily has learned to live with her depression. It is my hope that by working through this workbook, you will find the same hope, solutions, and happiness that Emily and many others have found.

So, what is this workbook about? It's about helping you manage your mood so it won't manage you. In the process, you will see how drug and alcohol use affect your mood and depression, and most important, what you need to do so you feel better. I hope that is what happens for you.

What's in a Mood?

Depression is a word we hear often. It describes a feeling we have in reaction to a situation. Everything from, "Oh my God, I am so depressed, I totally hate my biology teacher," to "I cannot believe my best friend totally dissed me." The depression we feel is often more serious than the depression we talk about. The point is, depression as a feeling is a normal part of everyone's life. It is normal to feel depressed when difficult or sad things happen. On the other hand, depression as a mood disorder is a completely different thing.

Depression as a mood disorder may not be in reaction to anything in particular. One of the most frustrating things about having a mood disorder is people constantly asking, "What are you depressed about?" Or even worse, all those helpful people who love to say, "You have it made. You don't have anything to be depressed about!" It is hard to explain to people that when you have a mood disorder, you probably aren't depressed about anything specific. But, at the same time, you are depressed about lots of stuff in general. This mood can make you cry or become cranky and irritable.

We will talk about two types of depression in this workbook: major depression and mild depression. *Major depression* can disrupt daily activities like going to school, studying, concentrating, sleeping, working, eating, and socializing with others. *Mild depression* or *dysthymia* is when you simply don't feel good. You feel cranky and depressed most of the time.

Tracking Your Mood

Sometimes, to understand your mood, you need to track it. This can help you see patterns in your mood. For example, you might find that your mood is worse during certain seasons, like around certain anniversary dates of someone's death. Some females learn that their mood is strongly influenced by their menstrual cycles. Tracking your mood will help you see when you are feeling better and if your medication and treatment are working.

A mood calendar and a mood scale are two good ways to track your mood. Both can be found in Activity 1, *Tracking Your Mood*.

 **Complete Activity 1**

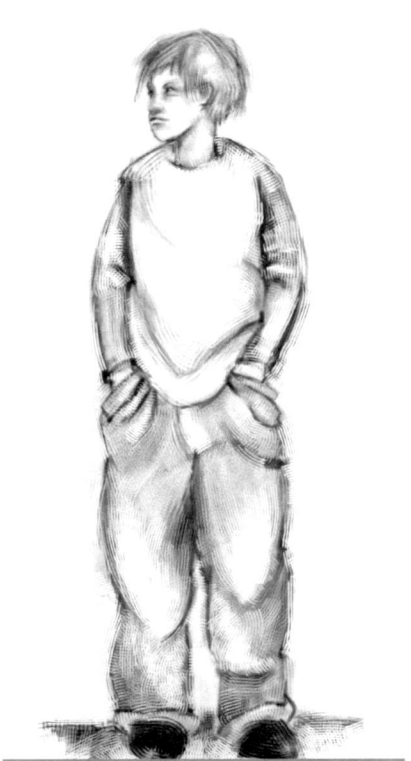

TRACKING YOUR MOOD

Name: _____

My Mood Calendar

DIRECTIONS: The first way to track your mood is to use a mood calendar for two weeks. Filling out the calendar is simple and will only take a few minutes. Three or four times a day, chart how you are feeling.

If you are feeling okay, put an arrow pointing up ↑.

If you are feeling really bad, put two arrows pointing down ↓↓.

Try to make charting your moods a habit. To help you with this, track your mood at the same times every day. If you forget to track your mood one day, fill out the calendar at night before you go to bed. But it's best to do it throughout the day because it will be more exact. For two weeks, carry this calendar with you at all times.

		7 A.M.	9 A.M.	11 A.M.	1 P.M.	3 P.M.	5 P.M.	7 P.M.	9 P.M.	11 P.M.
WEEK 1	Mon.									
	Tues.									
	Wed.									
	Thurs.									
	Fri.									
	Sat.									
	Sun.									
WEEK 2	Mon.									
	Tues.									
	Wed.									
	Thurs.									
	Fri.									
	Sat.									
	Sun.									

Activity 1 continued on next page

My Mood Scale

DIRECTIONS: The second way to track your mood is to use a mood scale. This is when you rate your mood on a scale of 1 to 10. The number 1 means that your mood is terrible and could not get any worse. The number 10 means your mood is great—you couldn't be doing any better. Most likely, you'll rate yourself somewhere between 1 and 10. When asked to rate your mood, simply circle the number.

1. What is your mood right now?

    1   2   3   4   5   6   7   8   9   10

2. What is the best your mood has been in the last week?

    1   2   3   4   5   6   7   8   9   10

    What day was this? _____

    What was going on that made you feel so good?

    _____

3. What is the worst your mood has been during the previous week?

    1   2   3   4   5   6   7   8   9   10

    What day was this? _____

    What was going on that made you feel so bad?

    _____

4. Last week, did you have more good days (or moments) or more bad days (or moments)? (circle one)

              Good   Bad

How Will You Know if Your Mood Is Better?

What does it mean to feel better? Some people have felt so bad for so long that feeling bad starts to feel normal. You may think that if you get help with your mood, then the bad feelings will disappear right away. That would be great! However, that is not the way it is. Everyone has bad days and feelings. But you will know you are starting to feel better when

- you still have bad days, but you don't have as many

- the bad days are not as bad as they were before

- bad moments don't always turn into bad hours, days, or weeks

There are a few things that put you at risk for depression:

1. **Genetic Makeup.** Mood problems tend to run in families. If your parents have mood disorders, you have a better chance of having one.

2. **The Brain's Reaction to Chronic Stress and Trauma.** Traumatic events can trigger depression. When the brain is overloaded with stress and trauma for a long period of time, sometimes this stress creates changes in brain chemistry.

3. **Hormonal Changes.** Hormone production affects neurotransmitters that then affect your mood. Big hormone changes taking place in your body can produce strong moods or rapidly changing moods.

4. **Mood-Altering Chemicals.** Mood-altering chemicals (chemicals that give you a high or a buzz) produce that high by affecting brain chemistry and manipulating the function of neurotransmitters. The younger someone's brain, the more vulnerable it is to mood-altering chemicals. The more vulnerable the brain, the more likely that use of mood-altering chemicals can contribute to the onset of a mood disorder.

5. **Being Sad a lot as a Child.** Some people are born being more sensitive to criticism and pain, overly anxious, more likely to worry, or always expecting the worst.

6. **Childhood Experiences that Are Hard to Deal With.** Some children have a hard time dealing with things such as changes, moves, the divorce of their parents, best friends leaving, and pets dying. Children who struggle with these things often are more at risk to be depressed as teenagers.

To discover what your own risk factors are, do Activity 2, *Risky Business— My Risk Factors.*

 Complete Activity 2

RISKY BUSINESS—MY RISK FACTORS

Name: _____

DIRECTIONS: Answer the following questions about risk factors. If you don't know the answer to the question or it doesn't apply to you, leave it blank.

1. Family History

The more people in your family who are or who have been depressed, the more you are at risk. When we talk about family, we mean your mom, dad, siblings, grandparents, cousins, aunts, and uncles. If possible, have your parents help you with this exercise. Complete the questions as best as you can.

a. Who in your immediate family is being or has been treated for depression?

_____

_____

b. Who on your mom's side of the family is being or has been treated for depression?

_____

c. Who on your dad's side of the family is being or has been treated for depression?

_____

d. Who has not been treated or diagnosed, but family members think probably were or are depressed?

_____

_____

Activity 2 continued on next page

2. Stress and Trauma

Think about some of the things that have been difficult for you in your life and answer the following questions.

Stress is experienced when things happen that you are not sure how to deal with.

a. What things have happened recently that have caused you stress?

_____

_____

_____

b. What things have been stressful for you in the past?

_____

_____

_____

c. What kinds of things have caused you ongoing stress? (For example, family conflicts, struggles with schoolwork, or problems with friends.)

_____

_____

_____

Trauma is an event or situation that causes great distress and disruption.

d. What things have happened recently that were traumatic for you?

_____

_____

_____

Activity 2 continued on next page

e. What things have happened earlier in your life that were traumatic for you?

_____

_____

f. Who have you talked to about these things?

_____

_____

3. Hormonal Changes

a. What is your date of birth? _____

b. Have you recently gone through growth spurts or noticed changes in your body that are due to hormones like facial and body hair or changes in your voice?

   ○ Yes ○ No

If yes, explain your body changes.

_____

_____

c. How old were you when you started going through puberty?

_____

d. If you are a female, do you notice changes in your mood connected to your menstrual cycle?

   ○ Yes   ○ No

If so, what kinds of changes have you noticed?

_____

_____

Activity 2 continued on next page

4. Alcohol or Other Drug Use

a. Are you currently using alcohol?

    ○ Yes   ○ No

b. What age were you when you started drinking?

_____

c. How often do you drink?

_____

d. How many drinks do you have when you drink?

_____

e. What is the most alcohol you have consumed at one time?

_____

f. Are you currently using pot or any other mood-altering substance?

    ○ Yes   ○ No

g. What substances (including pot) have you used?

_____

_____

h. How often do you use these substances?

_____

_____

i. How much pot do you use?

_____

_____

Activity 2 continued on next page

j. When was the last time you used pot or any other substance?

_____

k. Does anyone in your family drink too much or use mood-altering substances?

○ Yes   ○ No

5. Childhood Sadness

a. Do you remember being sad, unhappy, or moody as a child?

○ Yes   ○ No

Describe how you felt.

_____

_____

b. Take a look at family photos and pay close attention to pictures of yourself. What do you notice?

_____

_____

_____

c. Ask family members what they remember about your mood as a child. Write down what they say.

_____

_____

_____

_____

_____

Activity 2 continued on next page

6. Experiences that Were Hard to Deal With

As you look back on your life, what things did you find hard to deal with? Write down two experiences that you would be willing to share and discuss with others.

a. Experience 1:

I remember when I was _____ years old and this happened:

_____

_____

_____

_____

_____

_____

_____

b. Experience 2:

I remember when I was _____ years old and this happened:

_____

_____

_____

_____

_____

_____

_____

THE PHYSICAL DIMENSION
OF DEPRESSION

THE PHYSICAL DIMENSION OF DEPRESSION

Depression is a direct result of what is going on with brain chemistry (the physical part). Brain chemistry controls many things like mood, perception, concentration, anxiety, temper, and emotions. For people who are depressed, the brain chemicals that are responsible for regulating mood are not working right. It's like a four-cylinder car engine working on only two cylinders. These brain chemicals are called neurotransmitters.

Activity 3, *More than Moody: My Physical Symptoms,* lists some of the physical symptoms of depression.

 **Complete Activity 3**

MORE THAN MOODY: MY PHYSICAL SYMPTOMS

 Name: _____

DIRECTIONS: Read the symptoms below and check the ones that you have noticed in yourself lately. Write down other symptoms you have noticed that aren't on the list.

My Physical Symptoms

○ feeling tired even though you have gotten enough sleep

○ not being able to sleep even though you are tired

○ not being able to concentrate or focus

○ feeling like little things are too much trouble or effort

○ not having interest in doing things you used to enjoy

○ stress-related physical problems like headaches, stomachaches, or aches or pains that are hard to explain or identify

○ losing your appetite or eating even when you are not really hungry

○ not smiling or showing emotions in your face or with your body language (commonly referred to as flat effect)

Other symptoms:

_____

_____

_____

_____

Tips on Coping with Depression

Many people do not recognize the physical symptoms of depression. Since depression does have a physical base, there are things that have to happen so you can get your body feeling better. Besides medication prescribed by your medical doctor, here are other things that will help you feel better.

Get Some Sleep

Did you know that most of the serotonin that you need for a day is produced in the last two hours of a sleep cycle? Serotonin is an important chemical (neurotransmitter) that does many things in your brain including regulating your mood and helping you deal with anxiety. Some research even suggests that up to 75 percent of the serotonin your body needs during the course of a day is produced at this time. Now, here's the important thing to remember: it's the sleep cycle that produces serotonin. Naps do not count. If you do not get close to eight hours of sleep, work on trying to get more sleep.

Having trouble getting to sleep at night? Try these things:

- Drink milk before you go to bed. It's true, milk will help you sleep. It actually produces a sleep hormone that will help you relax. Don't like milk or are lactose intolerant? Then eat turkey. It is another great source for this hormone.

- Your body pays attention to cues that tell it if it is time to sleep or time to gear up for another activity. This is called cued behavior. One of the cues that tells your body it is time to sleep is when you crawl into bed. Many teens lay or sit in their bed to read, study, watch TV, or talk on the phone. When you do this, your body gets confused. If you are having trouble falling asleep, do not use your bed for any activity but sleeping.

- Lay off the caffeine. Even drinking caffeine earlier in the day can affect evening sleep. For example, stop drinking soda after lunch.

- Stop taking naps. Naps (even ones taken in study hall) mess up the body sleep clock.

- Try to keep your sleep patterns regular. Your body hates it when you change your sleep patterns. It has a hard time constantly readjusting.

- Give yourself fifteen to thirty minutes before you go to bed at night to wind down. This means you need to avoid activities that get your mind or body all revved up. For example, don't exercise right before going to bed or fight with a friend or boyfriend/girlfriend online or on the phone.

- Talk to your doctor if you still can't sleep.

Take Your Vitamin B

The more we learn about the brain, the more we understand the connection between what we eat and how our brain functions. Vitamin B is an energizing vitamin and should be taken in the morning, not later in the day. Our body needs complex vitamin B when it is under stress. The more stress, the more vitamin B our body needs. Good sources of vitamin B include whole grains, meat, low-fat dairy products, and leafy greens. By the way, alcohol kills vitamin B. When our body uses up all our vitamin B, then it depletes our serotonin and this impacts our mood. What should you do? Take a complex vitamin B daily. This vitamin is nontoxic. Your body uses what it needs and passes the rest.

Eat a Balanced Diet

Certain types of foods help our brain. Protein is the nutrient that the brain uses when it is trying to learn. Complex carbohydrates change our glucose levels which, in turn, affect serotonin production. In fact, if you checked your serotonin blood levels 15 minutes after eating a serving of complex carbohydrates, your serotonin blood levels would actually go up. This is why some people become cranky when they are hungry and their blood sugar dips. Kids with mood meltdowns say, "I feel better when I get something to eat." Eating is a simple way to improve mood and prevent mood problems. Try eating a serving of complex carbohydrates when you feel overwhelmed by your mood. Examples include baked potatoes, whole wheat pasta, breads, crackers, milk, and nuts. If you love junk food, that's okay, just try to add something nutritious to each meal.

Exercise

Exercise might be the last thing you want to do when you are depressed, but it has to be done. Get at least 20 minutes of exercise a day—and walking to and from class does not count. Find an activity that you enjoy like in-line skating, biking, swimming, running, or playing soccer or basketball.

Do Not Use Alcohol or Other Drugs

I will go into much more detail later in this workbook. But the bottom line is: no alcohol or other drugs.

• STEPHANIE'S STORY •

Hi, my name's Stephanie and I started going to therapy during my junior year. I was very depressed after my parents got divorced. It took a long time to figure out how to handle my mood. I really had to learn a whole different way of reacting to my feelings. When I start to get bummed out, I ask myself questions like: "Am I sleeping okay? Am I eating well? Am I stressed out at school? Am I getting sick?" Managing my mood is always more difficult when I am run down. Sometimes I have to give myself permission to feel badly, especially when I am tired or stressed out. I don't have to be afraid of my mood. I just have to take care of it.

In Activity 4, *My Plan for Managing My Physical Recovery,* you will list goals to help you handle your physical recovery.

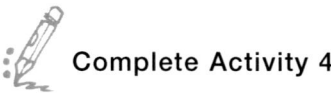 **Complete Activity 4**

MY PLAN FOR MANAGING MY PHYSICAL RECOVERY

Name: _____

DIRECTIONS: Now that you know five different ways to help manage the physical symptoms of your depression, name one thing you plan to do different under each category. If you do not feel ready to commit to major changes, think about small changes you can make in each of these areas.

Get Some Sleep

_____

_____

Take Your Vitamin B

_____

_____

Eat a Balanced Diet

_____

_____

Exercise

_____

_____

Do Not Use Alcohol or Other Drugs

_____

_____

What About Medication?

If you are depressed, what's going on in your brain is controlling how you feel physically, how you are thinking, and how you are feeling emotionally. Sometimes, medication prescribed by a doctor will help fix what is going on in your brain. Before you say something negative about taking medication, keep this in mind: it might be a way for you to begin feeling better. While some people manage their mood without it, others need the medication to feel better. Keep on reading. It will help you make an important decision about whether or not to take medication.

What Does the Medication Do?

New knowledge about how the brain works has brought about new medications that work for depression. Doctors will prescribe medication according to the symptoms you have. Different types of medications work different neurotransmitters in the brain. Prozac, Zoloft, and Paxil are commonly prescribed medications that target serotonin. In simple terms, these medications make the serotonin work more efficiently so it can do what it is supposed to do better.

Will I Have Side Effects?

Side effects can occur with any medication. Because you are taking the medication, you might have a headache, an upset stomach, dry mouth, feel groggy, have problems sleeping, or be more cranky or irritable than you were before you started taking the medication. Chances are, however, you won't have any side effects at all.

Who Should I Talk to about Medication?

Only a medical doctor or psychiatrist can prescribe medication. Find someone who

- you are comfortable with and can talk to

- explains things in a way you can understand

- knows teenagers, will listen to you, and give you medication choices

- knows how substance abuse and drinking can affect your mood and medications

- can answer your medication questions

Figuring out if medication is a good choice for you is difficult. Activity 5, *Is Medication a Good Choice for Me?*, might help you in your decision.

 Complete Activity 5

IS MEDICATION A GOOD CHOICE FOR ME?

Name: _____

DIRECTIONS: Read each statement and check True or False for each one.

1. You have been dealing with your mood for quite some time, and it does not seem to be getting better on its own.

    ○ True   ○ False

2. You have done things to try to make this mood better, but nothing you have done has worked.

    ○ True   ○ False

3. You find that you are discouraged and feel like giving up because your mood is getting the best of you.

    ○ True   ○ False

4. You have people in your family who have had depression and who have felt much better when they went on medication.

    ○ True   ○ False

5. Your mood is causing problems for you at school, with friends, or with your family.

    ○ True   ○ False

6. You have times when you feel so bad that you have thought about suicide.

    ○ True   ○ False

Activity 5 continued on next page

7. You have talked to a counselor and do not feel better.

    ○ True   ○ False

8. You have given up using drugs and alcohol, and your mood still has not improved.

    ○ True   ○ False

How many statements did you mark as true? _____

How many statements did you mark as false? _____

If you marked any of the statements as true, here is something to think about: You know what you feel like without medication. You won't know what you will feel like on medication until you give it a try.

How Will I Know if My Medication Is Working?

Most people do not know exactly what to expect when they start taking medication. Everyone is different. Some people are afraid it will put them in an annoyingly good mood or change their personality, or even make it impossible for them to have bad feelings or cry. In fact, it really won't do any of these things. It usually works gradually over three to six weeks. The main thing you will probably notice is that little things that used to bother you a lot won't bother you as much anymore. You might get annoyed, but you don't stay that way long. You might find that you just feel more like you can handle things and feel less overwhelmed. You will still have moods, but they might be more predictable, less extreme, and easier for you to control. For example, your medication won't make you stop fighting with your parents, but it might make it easier for you not to fight with them. It will not make choices for you, but it might make it easier for you to make choices you feel good about. These things happen gradually, over a period of weeks. It won't change who you are, it just will help you be who you were before the depression took over your mood.

What if I Don't Like It?

If you do not like the medication or feel it is not helping you, you can talk to your doctor about taking you off of it. Never stop taking medication without talking to your doctor first.

Will I Have to Take It Forever?

The answer to this question is, "It depends." Some people, especially those with a long history of serious mood problems, might need to take medications for a very long time. However, many young people take medication until their mood is stable, until the stress in their life has leveled off, until they have been clean from alcohol and other drugs, until they have solid coping skills and good support systems, and until their adolescent hormone surges even out. Many young people are able to gradually discontinue medication and do just fine. If the signs of depression return, medication is used to help them when they need it.

If You Decide to Take Medication

After you begin taking your medication, be patient. Chances are, you may not feel better right away. In fact, the medication will probably take three to six weeks to actually work. I know that when you do not feel well, a few weeks can seem like forever. Be patient.

Dosage is another issue. Doctors usually start with a lower dose and work up from there. This helps minimize side effects. Dosage varies from one medication to the next. What would be considered a high dose of Paxil, for example, would be a very small dose of Zoloft. If you have any questions, ask your doctor about what the average doses are.

Finding the right medication or the right combination of medication may take some time. Because everyone is different, your doctor may have you try a few medications before settling on one. It's not easy being patient, but just hang in there.

Take Your Medication as Prescribed

It will be impossible to see if your medication is helping you if you do not take it regularly. Work out a routine to remind yourself to take it daily. For example, if you take your medication when you get up in the morning, add the medication to your morning routine by placing your prescription bottle next to or on top of your toothpaste tube.

Ask Your Doctor

If you have any questions about your medication, ask your doctor. He or she is the one with the answers. Friends, parents, your basketball coach, and your aunt may all have opinions, but the doctor is the one with the correct answers. Talk to your doctor about side effects. Your doctor might have you take your medication at a different time of day or change your dose.

Tell your doctor what you think about your medication. You are the only one who knows how you truly feel. If you don't like the way it makes you feel, talk about it. Let the doctor know if it is helping in some ways, but not others. Do not just quit taking the medication without your doctor's approval.

If the medication has helped your mood and you want to try to go off the medication, you have a better chance of keeping your mood stable if you go off gradually and decrease your dose slowly. Once again, your doctor will help you do this.

Depression Medication and Drugs or Alcohol Do Not Mix

At the very least, alcohol and other drug use will prevent your medication from working. The drug use may cause symptoms that look like a mood disorder, and you won't be able to tell if the medication is helping. At worst, the medication mixed with alcohol or other drugs can be dangerous or even deadly. It's a really bad idea.

Why No Drugs?

Dave, a sixteen-year-old recovering pot head with a serious mood problem, came strolling into my office one day with a T-shirt that said: "Reality is for people who can't handle their drugs."

When I asked him about the shirt, he looked at me, smiled, and said, "That would be me, right?" That about says it all. The reality is that you have a mood problem, and any use of alcohol or other mood-altering substance is going to make it impossible to stabilize your mood. When you are really honest with yourself, you will know this is true.

• GILLIAN'S STORY •

Hi, I'm Gillian. It's hard to say when my depression really began. Because I was really scared of social situations, I was always very quiet. I would think to myself, "I am not going to talk to those people because there is no reason they would want to talk to me." Looking back, I see how twisted my thinking was. If someone said "hi" to me, I would convince myself they were just being nice and didn't really want to talk to me. If they invited me to go somewhere, I would convince myself that they did not really want me along.

Things started to spiral out of control. Just like other teenagers, a social life was one of my top priorities. The problem was that I did not know how to be social because I had always been so afraid and isolated from the world. I did not let anyone in. I was dealing with depression and social anxiety alone.

Then one day I found alcohol. It became my miracle drug. No other substance could even compare to how alcohol made me feel. I no longer just stood there quietly. Now I was the life of the party. When I drank, my personality changed. I was not the same person at all. I felt like I was normal and part of the group. Most of all, I felt like I belonged. On the weekends when I was drinking, all my inhibitions left. All my anxiety, anger, and darkness disappeared. But then, Monday morning would come along and my real world would come crashing back. I wouldn't even say hi to the people that I had spent all weekend with in a drunken binge. So, I decided to start drinking every day. I did that for a year and a half. Was I happy? I can't say that I wasn't. For this period of time, alcohol seemed to be the solution to all my problems. It was my miracle drug.

But then I found it harder and harder to reach that state of happiness that I once had found so easily. I had to drink more and more to get a buzz. Eventually, I would drink and pass out before ever reaching that state I was looking for. Alcohol stopped working. I had lost the only thing that made me happy. That is when everything collapsed. Now I felt worse about myself than ever. I didn't know it until the alcohol was gone, but I had fallen deeper into depression. I wanted to die and I was more than willing to be the one to kill myself. But I didn't. To get better, I had to be real and that was not easy. I had my ups and downs, short periods of being sober followed by binges with alcohol.

I couldn't get past my pattern of negative behavior on my own. Counseling and medication helped. When I was finally able to think straight, I listened to what people were telling me. Then I thought about my own actions and understood what they meant. I realize now that my drinking was my way of medicating my feelings. The depression went away with medication, therapy, and time. I still struggle with social anxiety, though. I never learned how to become social with others because I was too worried about being afraid. When I was drinking, I wasn't learning because it was not me being social, it was the alcohol.

I have just finished my first year of college. I have friends now and am not deathly afraid of social situations. I can go to parties without drinking. However, I only reached this point in my life by taking risks.

Today, I can identify what I need to do to be the person I want to be. That means that I have to take care of myself by monitoring my mood. If I begin to slip toward depression, I ask for help if I need it. I have to make healthy choices about using any mood-altering substances. This means I can't drink. There is a long road ahead of me to become the person I want to be and make the choices that I would like myself to make. Am I perfect? No, but I am learning and getting better every day. I have made it this far so I am not going to give up. I am going to reach my goals and I am going to be okay.

Gillian's story is a real-life example of how mood and alcohol problems make each worse when combined. Can you relate to any of Gillian's story?

Activity 6, *What Happens When Someone Who Is Depressed Uses Drugs or Alcohol?,* provides some answers about using while depressed.

 **Complete Activity 6**

WHAT HAPPENS WHEN SOMEONE WHO IS DEPRESSED USES DRUGS OR ALCOHOL?

Name: _____

DIRECTIONS: The seven facts listed here will help you answer the question, "What happens when someone who is depressed uses drugs or alcohol?" Some of the facts include a question-and-answer portion. Answer as best as you can.

Fact 1

Just a little bit of drugs or alcohol can cause a large amount of damage to your mood.

One of the first things I hear from young people when I ask them about their use of mood-altering substances is, "I don't use a lot." I realize that in some cases this is true and in other cases it is a lie. You don't have to use a lot to screw up your mood.

Having a mood disorder implies that your mood is vulnerable—that means it can be affected easily. You don't have good control over your mood when little things make you angry or drive you to tears. Introducing a substance into your brain that takes control over your mood is not a good idea. Chances are since you have been using, your mood has gotten worse. You may not see it, but other people surely will.

a. In what ways has drinking or using mood-altering chemicals affected your mood? (check the ways that you can relate to most)

○ I become irritated easily.

○ I get angry.

○ I get emotional.

○ other _____

Activity 6 continued on next page

Fact 2

There is a reason why people with mood disorders like to use mood-altering chemicals, and it's not a good reason.

When I ask people why they use alcohol or other drugs, they often tell me, "I just use because I like it." They are being honest. It is obvious that they like it. That's the whole reason they got in trouble with it. The real question is, "Why do you like it so much?"

If you have a mood disorder, you are probably unhappy and uncomfortable with your mood. Drugs help you escape from that discomfort. If they actually fixed the mood, maybe this would not be a problem. However, while drug use calms the mood while you are under the influence, the moment you are no longer under the influence, your mood will be worse than it was before you used.

Let's take alcohol, for example. Generally, two alcoholic drinks will raise your serotonin level. This provides an immediate mood reward when you drink. However, for every drink over two, the serotonin level dips. As a result, your alcohol-induced mood becomes worse the more you drink. You then become sad, tired, or angry. The next day, your serotonin level rebounds. While it is doing this, your mood becomes even worse. It may even take days for your serotonin level to straighten itself out. In the meantime, you might remember how good that first drink made you feel and become drawn to the idea of drinking again.

So, of course, people who are depressed or anxious like to drink. Does this solve their mood problems? No, but it sure makes drinking seem terribly rewarding. Eventually, the drinking causes even more mood problems than before. You may find yourself drinking even more as you try to control these mood problems.

a. What do you like about how drugs and alcohol make you feel?

_____

_____

_____

Activity 6 continued on next page

b. Have you ever drank or used drugs to help you feel more comfortable socially? If yes, explain.

_____

_____

_____

c. What types of feelings have you tried to avoid or get away from by drinking or using drugs?

_____

_____

_____

Fact 3

It's hereditary. If someone else in your family has a mood disorder, using mood-altering substances when you are young can increase your risk of a more serious mood disorder at a very early age.

Mood disorders stem from brain chemistry. When you have vulnerable brain chemistry, using substances that create highs by messing with brain chemistry is dangerous. In fact, recent research shows that people who begin using marijuana while they are adolescents have much higher incidents of mood disorders and other psychiatric problems in their late teens and early twenties.

a. Who in your family has had problems with their mood or with depression? Write their names and how they are related to you.

_____

_____

_____

_____

Activity 6 continued on next page

b. How old were you when you first experienced problems with your mood?

_____

Fact 4

Medication doesn't work right when you are using mood-altering chemicals.

Adolescents often know, but do not always like to admit to others, that there is something wrong with the way they feel. They can't concentrate in school, are negative and irritable, and might feel like they are going crazy. Doctors prescribe medication for these symptoms. Many parents, teachers, and other adults are eager for the teens to take these medications because they think things will get better. The only problem is, if mood-altering chemicals are being used with any consistency or frequency, the substances prevent the medication from working.

Maybe you've been in this situation yourself. If you have, you know what happens next. Everyone starts complaining that the medication is not working. Another trip to the doctor and the medicine gets changed, the dose gets adjusted, but nothing changes. So the doctor starts adding new medications to the old medications, trying to find the quick, easy solutions to your mood. The truth is that the medications are not going to work until you get rid of the mood-altering chemicals. Potent substances like cocaine, crack, or crystal meth assault your brain with powerful neuro-transmitter-altering chemicals. These neurotransmitters are responsible for regulating your mood. If you use them all up for a trip, or a role, or a high, they will not be there to regulate your mood when the high is gone.

Withdrawal from any drug is the opposite of what the drug does when you're under its influence. For example, if cocaine makes you feel incredibly good when you're on it, then you are going to feel incredibly bad when the drug effect wears off. Your mood will take a dive. No medication your doctor can give you is going to help you feel better while you're using substances that keep your mood on a roller coaster.

Activity 6 continued on next page

a. Are you currently taking medication prescribed to help you with your mood or behavior?

      ○ Yes   ○ No

If so, what is the name of the medication?

_____

b. Write what you know about how alcohol or other drug use interacts with the medication you are taking.

_____

_____

_____

c. If you do not know how alcohol and other drugs interact with your medication, how can you find out?

_____

_____

_____

Fact 5

Using mood-altering substances, especially pot, will rob you of the motivation you need to do what it will take to manage your mood.

If you want to take control of your mood and feel better, it's going to take a lot of hard work. You can have the best intentions to "do better," "straighten out your mood," and "fix your relationships," but the motivation goes right out the window when you get high.

I have known many pot smokers who assure me that weed does not take their bad mood away. They say they can still feel their mood, it just makes them not care as much that they feel like crap.

Activity 6 continued on next page

If you feel like crap, you should care. You should not accept this as the way to get through your day or week or entire adolescence. You have to care that you feel like crap, and you don't have to feel like crap. You can get better, but it will take some effort.

a. How has your motivation to do something changed since you started using drugs or alcohol?

_____

_____

_____

_____

_____

Fact 6

You have to experience your mood in order to manage it.

If you do not allow yourself to experience your mood, you will never learn about it or be able to control it. Mood-altering chemicals separate you from your mood. You do not need to be separated from it. You need to learn to master it.

a. How do alcohol and other drugs separate you from your mood?

_____

_____

_____

_____

_____

_____

_____

Activity 6 continued on next page

Fact 7

It does not matter what came first, the drugs and alcohol or the mood disorder. Both have to be taken care of if you are going to feel better.

I hear adolescents often say, "My real problem is I am depressed. I think that if I can get some help with my depression, then my drug use (or drinking) won't be such a big deal. I was depressed before I started using." I also hear the parent version. It goes something like this: "I am sure he's smoking a little pot. I think all kids go through that. But I really don't think that's his main problem. I really think he's depressed and if we can get to the bottom of that, I think the pot use will take care of itself."

I also get the million dollar question, "What do you think is the main problem, her mood or her drug use? Which one should we deal with first?" It doesn't really matter which came first. The main problem is that they now go hand in hand.

Maybe you started using drugs and drinking because you were depressed or because something terrible happened to you. Maybe you're depressed because you have been using drugs and bad things have happened because of your drug use. At this point, both your mood and drug use have to be dealt with at the same time if you are going to feel better. Treating your depression might make it easier to give up drugs, but it is not going to make your drug use go away. Getting off drugs will help your depression, but it probably won't make it go away.

a. How has your mood affected your use of alcohol and other drugs? For example, when you are discouraged, do you use alcohol or other drugs?

_____

_____

_____

_____

Activity 6 continued on next page

_____

_____

_____

_____

_____

b. When you are using alcohol or other drugs, how does it affect your mood? Do you feel happier or more calm at first? How do you feel the next day? Please explain.

_____

_____

_____

_____

_____

_____

_____

_____

_____

_____

_____

_____

THE COGNITIVE DIMENSION
OF DEPRESSION

THE COGNITIVE DIMENSION OF DEPRESSION

Simply put, when people become physically depressed, the brain's thought process is affected. That thought process then affects feelings. This cognitive process is often called negative thinking.

One example of a negative thinker is Eeyore from the Winnie the Pooh stories. Eeyore approaches the world in a different way than the other characters. A dark cloud follows him around. He expects bad things to happen to him. He thinks the bad things that happen to him are far worse than those that happen to others. Eeyore sees the dark lining in any silver cloud. This is clearly shown in one story when Eeyore's friends planned a birthday party for him. Instead of being happy about it, he said, "They are going to give me a birthday party, and probably no one will come." Only Eeyore could turn something positive like a birthday party into something negative.

The longer negative thinking goes on, the easier it is for the brain to respond negatively. Eventually, the brain automatically reacts negatively to everything, even though you may not even realize it. Negative thoughts can control every part of your life and affect how you look at the world and your life experiences. Negative thoughts contribute to feelings of depression.

Some symptoms of negative thinking are

- being extremely irritable

- being sarcastic

- being critical of others

- being cranky

- having small things bother you a lot

- often thinking things are stupid and annoying

Recognizing and Changing Negative Thought Patterns

Negative thinking creates a negative mood. If every little unpleasant situation you have begins to affect your mood throughout the day or week, it won't take long for you to have many bad days or bad weeks in a row. Soon, life can begin to feel hopeless. There are five different categories of negative thought patterns for adolescents:

1. Negative thoughts about your life

2. Negative thoughts about yourself

3. Negative thoughts about others

4. All-or-nothing negative thinking

5. Negative thoughts about the future

To overcome negative thinking patterns, first you have to be able to recognize these thinking patterns. Then you must challenge negative thoughts (N.T.s) and replace them with more accurate realistic thoughts (R.T.s). Activity 7, *Picking Your Perspective,* will help you begin to change your thinking.

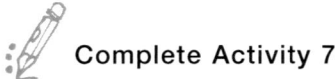 **Complete Activity 7**

PICKING YOUR PERSPECTIVE

Name: _____

DIRECTIONS: Each category contains a list of negative thoughts (N.T.s) and realistic replacement thoughts (R.T.s). For each category, circle the negative thoughts that you can relate to most. Then answer the questions that follow.

CATEGORY ONE: Negative Thoughts About Your Life

N.T. If one bad thing happens, the rest of the day is going to be terrible.

R.T. It stinks that this happened, but it is just one small part of my day.

N.T. Bad things happen more often to me than to other people.

R.T. Bad things happen to everybody and nobody likes it when it happens to them.

N.T. Life is just crappy and you can't do anything about it.

R.T. Crappy things happen, but life isn't crappy.

N.T. Everything is boring.

R.T. Some things are not as much fun as other things. This doesn't mean they are boring, they just aren't as fun.

N.T. If ten good things happen and one bad thing happens, the one bad thing outweighs all the good things.

R.T. One thing went wrong today, but nine things went right.

N.T. My choices do not have any impact on my life.

R.T. I have a great deal of control over my life by the choices I make.

Activity 7 continued on next page

53

N.T.   Nothing ever goes right for me.

R.T.   Everything does not go right for me, but everything doesn't go wrong for me either.

N.T.   The worst-case scenario is always the most likely to happen.

R.T.   The worst-case scenario might be true, but there are other less negative ways it could happen too.

N.T.   Since bad things happen to me, I have to worry and think about them constantly.

R.T.   Worrying does not stop bad things from happening, but making better choices might.

1. Circle the N.T.s you can relate to most. Explain why you can relate to them.

   _____

   _____

   _____

   _____

   _____

2. What are some other negative thoughts about your life that creep into your mind?

   _____

   _____

   _____

   _____

   _____

Activity 7 continued on next page

3. What are some realistic replacement thoughts you can use next time your thinking becomes negative? The R.T.s listed on the previous pages can help you come up with new ideas.

_____

_____

_____

_____

_____

CATEGORY TWO: Negative Thoughts About Yourself

N.T. If others are smart and good looking, then that must mean that I am ugly and stupid.

R.T. He/she is smart and so am I. He/she is good looking and so am I.

N.T. I can't do anything right.

R.T. I don't do everything right, but I do lots of things right.

N.T. I'm stupid.

R.T. I'm not good at _____ (fill in a school subject).

N.T. I avoid things that are too hard for me to do.

R.T. I can deal with things that are hard to do.

1. Circle the N.T.s you can relate to most. Explain why you can relate to them.

_____

_____

_____

_____

Activity 7 continued on next page

2. What are some other negative thoughts about yourself that creep into your mind?

_____

_____

_____

_____

_____

3. What are some realistic replacement thoughts you can use next time you begin to beat yourself up with negative thinking? The R.T.s listed on the previous pages can help you come up with new ideas.

_____

_____

_____

_____

_____

_____

CATEGORY THREE: Negative Thoughts About Others

N.T. When other people are in a bad mood, it means they are mad at me.

R.T. Sometimes people are in a bad mood because they don't feel well or are worried about something. It has nothing to do with me.

N.T. If one person does not like me, it means that no one likes me.

R.T. Not everyone I meet is going to like me. It's just the way it is. That's not saying anything bad about me.

Activity 7 continued on next page

N.T. People are just stupid and annoying.

R.T. All people can be stupid and annoying some of the time, but everyone is not stupid and annoying all the time.

N.T. If people are quiet around me, it means they do not like me.

R.T. There are a lot of reasons why people are quiet that don't have anything to do with me. Sometimes people are just quiet because it's part of their personality.

N.T. People are always picking on me.

R.T. Some people pick on everyone and that includes me. Sometimes I think people are picking on me when they don't really mean anything by it.

N.T. You can't trust anyone.

R.T. You can't trust everyone, but you can trust some people. I can trust myself to determine who is trustworthy and who is not.

N.T. People are trying to make my life difficult.

R.T. Most people are too busy worrying about their life to be that focused on mine.

1. Circle the N.T.s you can relate to most. Explain why you can relate to them.

_____

_____

_____

_____

_____

_____

Activity 7 continued on next page

2. What are some other negative thoughts about others that creep into your mind?

_____

_____

_____

_____

_____

3. What are some realistic replacement thoughts you can use next time you begin to think negatively about others? The R.T.s listed on the previous pages can help you come up with new ideas.

_____

_____

_____

_____

_____

CATEGORY FOUR: All-or-Nothing Negative Thinking
(If everything is not perfect, then everything stinks.)

N.T. If something is not totally great, then it sucks.

R.T. This may not be great, but it's okay.

N.T. If one person is mean to me, then everyone is mean.

R.T. Some people are mean, everyone isn't.

N.T. If one thing is hard, then I give up on everything.

R.T. This is hard, but thank goodness, everything isn't this hard.

Activity 7 continued on next page

N.T. If I don't like something, then I hate it.

R.T. There are some things that I like better than others.

N.T. If you say or do one mean thing to me, then you are just mean.

R.T. I have to balance out the mean things with the nice things you have said or done. This way, I can decide if you are a nice person who sometimes says or does mean things or if you are a mean person.

N.T. If dinner does not taste great, then it's nasty.

R.T. This dinner may not taste great, but I've tasted worse.

N.T. If I can't have the most expensive shoes, then all other shoes are crappy.

R.T. These expensive shoes are awesome, but these other shoes are okay too.

1. Circle the N.T.s you can relate to most. Explain why you can relate to them.

   _____

   _____

   _____

   _____

2. What are some other all-or-nothing ideas that creep into your mind?

   _____

   _____

   _____

   _____

Activity 7 continued on next page

3. What are some realistic replacement thoughts you can use next time you begin to have this all-or-nothing thinking? The R.T.s listed in Category Four can help you come up with new ideas.

_____

_____

_____

_____

_____

_____

CATEGORY FIVE: Negative Thoughts About the Future
(If something bad happens now—even if it's not a very big thing—it will have a huge impact on what the future will look like.)

N.T. I feel rotten and will never feel any better.

R.T. I feel rotten now, but I won't always feel so bad.

N.T. If high school sucks, the rest of my life will suck too.

R.T. High school may be really bad sometimes, but the rest of my life won't look like my worst day in high school.

N.T. If the girl (or guy) I like does not like me, I probably won't ever be liked by anyone else.

R.T. This girl (or guy) does not like me, but that doesn't mean that other girls (or guys) won't like me.

N.T. If I can't pass this algebra test, I will probably never get a good grade in this class.

R.T. If I did not do well on this test, I can make up for it in other areas like preparing better for a quiz.

Activity 7 continued on next page

N.T. Nothing matters.

R.T. Lots of stuff matters.

N.T. It's no use.

R.T. What I do does matter.

N.T. Why bother?

R.T. I bother because it's my life and it does matter.

1. Circle the N.T.s you can relate to most. Explain why you can relate to them.

   _____

   _____

   _____

   _____

   _____

   _____

2. What are some other negative thoughts about the future that creep into your mind?

   _____

   _____

   _____

   _____

   _____

   _____

   _____

Activity 7 continued on next page

3. What are some realistic replacement thoughts you can use next time you begin to have negative thoughts about the future? The R.T.s listed in Category Five can help you come up with new ideas.

_____

_____

_____

_____

_____

_____

_____

_____

_____

Your Moods and Your Relationships

Negative thinking creates many problems in relationships. Friends may get burned out when you complain all the time. They might also feel that you make them more negative. So they may begin to distance themselves from you to protect their mood.

Negative moods can become all consuming. If you look at the world through doom-and-gloom glasses, that's all you will see, even when it is not there. For example, you might misinterpret someone's comment or how they look at you. You might start to feel insulted and disrespected. These things make it difficult (if not impossible) for others to be a good friend. Your negative mood can convince you that you have no friends, you can't trust others, and people are just too much trouble, so you withdraw. Your friends won't have a clue about why you are reacting this way, and they will pull back too.

Negative moods interfere with romantic relationships too. People are often most moody with people they are closest to. Females tend to be cranky or irritable while males become angry. These moods confuse people. A boyfriend or girlfriend may think you are mad at them even though it may just be your mood and have nothing to do with them. The boyfriend or girlfriend may feel bad because they want to help you feel better. They may even try to make you feel better. When that doesn't work, they become frustrated. Fights over "stupid" things happen.

Family relationships are also affected by negative moods. Let's face it, few people have perfect families. Young people love to complain about their families. Most parents can't do anything to please their teens. I talk to teens whose parents set fairly appropriate limits and rules for them. They tell me how controlling and out of touch their parents are. They believe they would not have the problems they do if their parents would lighten up. I also talk to teens whose parents set no limits and even go so far as to get high with their own kids. These teens tell me their parents are crazy, immature, and irresponsible. These teens also believe they wouldn't have problems if their parents would get a clue and take a stand.

The truth is, if you are depressed, you are cranky, irritable, and sad. This might be for reasons you don't understand, can't explain, or can't point out. When you don't know why your mood stinks, it is easy to blame it on your parents. Even though they may make you mad, hurt your feelings, or make you feel you can't do anything right, the fact is that your parents can't create a clinical condition known as depression. Your parents are just a convenient excuse for your mood. Blaming them is not going to make you feel better.

If you moved out of your home tomorrow and moved into a place of your own, you would take your mood with you. You might be happy that you have your own place and can set your own rules, but that does not mean your depression would disappear.

• DANNI'S STORY •

Danni began therapy with me when she was 15 years old. Her parents brought her to therapy because they knew she was smoking pot, and they were worried about her mood. They described her as negative, critical, and never happy. Danni talked during therapy, but she hardly ever smiled, never looked forward to anything, and described herself as "a cold-hearted bitch." She described her friends as superficial, materialistic, and drama queens. She mistreated and picked fights with her boyfriend. He could not please her no matter what he did. She smoked pot every day, couldn't stand her teachers, and thought school was stupid. She thought her only problems were her parents and high school. Everything about high school annoyed her.

Danni admitted that she didn't like her life and wanted things to get better. The only solution she saw was to graduate from high school, go to college, and get away from her family and all the other stupid people she knew. She was totally convinced that her mood was every-one else's fault. She promised herself she would quit smoking weed when she got there. So Danni graduated from high school and went to the college of her choice. Everything was new: new school, new friends, new boyfriend, new town, new classes, and new teachers. Everything was different but Danni. Her mood went along to college with her.

She smoked more weed, fought with her roommates, couldn't stand her teachers, didn't go to her college classes, and mistreated her boyfriend. She realized how badly she missed her family. This was the family that she could not wait to get away from and held responsible for all her problems.

Danni made it through one semester before she dropped out and came back to her family and therapy. When I asked her what happened, she said, "It really sucks when you realize how miserable you are and don't have your parents to blame." Unfortunately she lost a lot before she came to this realization. This was the start of Danni's recovery.

Activity 8, *Negative Moods and Relationships,* will help you discover how your negative moods have affected your family, friends, and romantic relationships.

 **Complete Activity 8**

NEGATIVE MOODS AND RELATIONSHIPS

Name: _____

DIRECTIONS: For each type of relationship listed below, answer the questions as best as you can.

1. Relationships with Friends

a. What types of comments have your friends made about your mood or attitude?

_____

_____

_____

_____

b. Have you ever noticed friends pulling away from you because of your mood or attitude?

○ Yes   ○ No

c. Give an example of when your friends pulled away from you because of your mood or attitude.

_____

_____

_____

d. Give an example of when you misinterpreted or misjudged someone because of your negative mood.

_____

_____

_____

Activity 8 continued on next page

e. When have your friends withdrawn from you because of your negative mood?

_____

_____

_____

_____

2. Romantic Relationships

a. Write down a time when you fought with a boyfriend, girlfriend, or a good friend over nothing just because you were in a bad mood.

_____

_____

_____

_____

b. Write down something your boyfriend, girlfriend, or good friend said about your mood.

_____

_____

_____

_____

c. How do your mood problems interfere with your friendships?

_____

_____

_____

_____

Activity 8 continued on next page

3. Family Relationships

Name three kinds of problems that your negative mood has created for your family.

a. _____

_____

_____

_____

b. _____

_____

_____

_____

c. _____

_____

_____

_____

Managing Your Mind

Since we know that depression and mood problems live in your mind, we know that part of the solution lies in managing your thought process. This is not an easy thing because negative thoughts become deeply fixed in the brain. It takes a lot of effort to change them. So that means you're in for a lot of hard work. Even though these are your thoughts and you can manage and control them, your brain will resist this change.

Change is difficult. Have you ever tried to change your jump shot or your tennis swing? At first it is very difficult because your brain has been trained to do it a certain way. You have to give a great deal of thought when you change something that you do automatically. When you first try to change, the old way will seem better. It probably will seem like it's hardly worth the effort to change. When you attempt to change your reactions to events in your life, it will be difficult. Your brain will go back to the old way of thinking because it seems most natural and comfortable. You have to make a big effort to think about things differently.

I often hear, "I can't help it; I can't control my thoughts." That just means that it is hard, not impossible. Managing your mood will become easier once you learn how to recognize your negative thinking patterns and replace negative thoughts with more realistic replacement thoughts.

Activity 9, *Overcoming the Negatives, What It Takes,* leads you through the four steps that will help you manage your mood and change your thinking patterns.

 **Complete Activity 9**

OVERCOMING THE NEGATIVES, WHAT IT TAKES

Name: _____

DIRECTIONS: There are four specific steps that you can take to help you overcome your negative thinking patterns. Read through each step and then answer the questions as best as you can.

Step One

Recognize Your Negative Thoughts

The first step to changing your mood is recognizing your negative thinking. You have probably been negatively overreacting for so long that you don't even realize you do it. Pay close attention to your negative thinking patterns. You cannot change those patterns until you realize they are happening. Be aware of those negative thoughts. You'll be surprised how many negative thoughts creep into your brain.

How often do you hear yourself complaining, criticizing, whining, insulting, or calling something (or someone) stupid? You need to monitor this negative talk.

a. First, think about some of the negative thoughts, words, or phrases that you use every day and write them down. (If you need more room for your answers, write them on a separate piece of paper.)

_____

_____

_____

_____

_____

_____

Activity 9 continued on next page

b. Second, keep track of how often you think or say these things in one day. Select one day when you will do this exercise. Put a check mark after each phrase you listed each time it pops out of your mouth. It's okay to add more phrases to the list.

c. If you force yourself to change your negative language, you will force yourself to rethink your negative reactions. The third step is to think of some less negative words or phrases you can use instead of the ones you listed on the previous page and write them below.

_____

_____

_____

_____

_____

_____

Step Two

Challenge Your Thought Patterns

Challenge your thought patterns. Ask yourself the following questions the next time you start reacting negatively to something.

1. What is really bothering me here?

2. Is it really that bad?

3. Does it make sense that I am having such a strong reaction to this situation?

4. Am I overreacting?

5. Is my reaction being driven more by my mood than by the reality of the situation?

6. What's going to happen next if I continue to dwell on this?

Activity 9 continued on next page

Step Three

Replace Your Negative Thought Patterns

Replace those extreme and negative thoughts. Ask yourself the following questions to help you replace your negative thoughts.

1. Is there another way to think about this situation?

2. Is there another, less negative way to look at what just happened here?

3. Can I at least consider the possibility that another less negative situation exists?

Step Four

Stop Your Negative Thoughts

The earlier you catch your negative thoughts, the easier they are to stop. One negative thought leads to many more. It is easier to stop one before it becomes ten. Get your brain involved in another activity. We call this a thought-stopping technique. You have to find something that keeps your brain busy, but not frustrated. When you feel like your head is spinning so fast that you can't stop, try one of these thought-stopping techniques:

• Count backward from twenty by twos.

• Count backward from thirty by threes.

• Put a rubber band on your wrist and snap it one time quickly.

• Take slow deep breaths into your nose and blow out through your mouth. Concentrate on your breathing.

• Distract yourself. Don't just sit there grooving on those negative thoughts listening to music that tells you how bad the world is. Distract yourself. Call a friend, watch a movie, or put on a different CD.

Activity 9 continued on next page

Which one of these four thought-stopping techniques are you going to try next time your negative thinking starts taking over? Write it down below, use it, then write down how it felt and if it worked.

a. Thought-stopping technique I'll use:

_____

_____

b. How it felt when I used this technique:

_____

_____

_____

_____

c. Did the thought-stopping technique stop the negative thinking? Why or why not?

_____

_____

_____

_____

_____

_____

_____

THE EMOTIONAL DIMENSION
OF DEPRESSION

Activity 10

Dealing with Feelings

PAGE 79

Activity 11

Ways to Make Your Mood Better

PAGE 89

THE EMOTIONAL DIMENSION OF DEPRESSION

Although depression is not a feeling, many feelings, including sadness, go along with it. There is a difference between sadness and depression. Many people think any kind of sadness is a bad thing. It's not. Sadness is a normal reaction to certain situations. It is normal to be sad if someone dies, hurts you, ends a relationship, or fights with you. When you get sad because of a life situation, it is not usually a problem and doesn't need to be analyzed or treated with medication.

If too many things happen to you that make you very sad in a short period of time, the stress that builds up may trigger depression or mood swings. So, sometimes, but not always, sad feelings can lead to depression. If that is the case, what created the sadness has to be looked at. The emotional part of depression involves much more than being just sad. Powerful and often frightening feelings come out. The scary thing about these feelings is that you might not know why you feel the way you do. These feelings come out of nowhere and take over your emotional world.

Activity 10, *Dealing with Feelings,* describes some of the feelings you may have when you're depressed.

 **Complete Activity 10**

DEALING WITH FEELINGS

Name: _____

DIRECTIONS: The feelings listed below are some of the most difficult to understand and live with. Read the descriptions of each feeling and answer the questions below as best as you can.

1. Helplessness

Often the feelings of depression come on so quickly that you feel helpless in changing them. As depression creeps in and takes over your world, you feel like a dark cloud is swallowing you up. Sometimes it is so hard to explain to others just how awful you feel. You may feel like you cannot control anything and are powerless.

a. Write down your feelings of helplessness.

_____

_____

_____

_____

_____

2. Hopelessness

Hopelessness is often connected to the physical part of depression like feeling tired, overwhelmed, or not having any energy or desire to do things that you know you need to do. Hopelessness is also connected to the cognitive part of depression. You may feel so lost in your negative thinking and reactions to the world that you feel hopeless. Hopelessness makes you think that no matter what you do, you won't be able to change things or make them better. In fact, you may have tried and failed to make changes and feel hopeless about that.

Activity 10 continued on next page

a. Describe a time when you experienced feelings of hopelessness.

_____

_____

_____

_____

3. Not Caring

The feelings of depression cause you to not care about things you used to care about. You stop enjoying things you used to enjoy. You don't worry about your safety. You simply don't care anymore. You are consumed with the feeling that nothing matters so there is no use in trying.

a. Give examples of things that you have stopped caring about.

_____

_____

_____

_____

4. Losing Your Joy and Your Passion

In depression, you lose the desire to enjoy life. You begin to lose interest in things that you used to be passionate about.

a. What types of things used to bring you joy but don't anymore?

_____

_____

_____

b. When was the last time you felt joy and happiness?

_____

Activity 10 continued on next page

5. Being Stuck in Sadness

In depression, you can't bounce back or recover from a bad situation—
you get stuck in sadness.

a. Do you feel you are stuck in sadness now?

○ Yes   ○ No

If so, how long have you felt this way?

_____

_____

_____

6. Losing Touch with Your Values

When you are depressed, you begin to be confused about what you
believe. You question or doubt the core of your soul and who you
are—you question your values, beliefs, and dreams. When you do
this, you begin to feel like you are wandering around lost.

a. What doubts have you had about your values or your beliefs?

_____

_____

_____

_____

b. What things have you done that go against your values or beliefs?

_____

_____

_____

_____

Activity 10 continued on next page

7. Feeling Overwhelmed

When you are depressed, the idea of doing the smallest tasks seems overwhelming. Things that used to be no big deal suddenly are too difficult to handle.

a. What simple tasks overwhelm you or stress you out?

_____

_____

_____

_____

Making Your Mood Better

Now that you understand the feelings of depression, it is time to learn how to deal with these feelings. When it feels like nobody else in the world has ever felt as bad as you do, it might help to know that millions of teens do feel sad and have overcome it. Here are just a few ways to help you overcome your mood in difficult times.

Remember That It Will Not Last Forever

Thank goodness that bad feelings come and go. They may last for a few moments, days, or weeks, but they will not last forever. When you are stuck in the middle of awful feelings, keep this in mind: When those bad feelings are gone and you look back on them, you'll probably say, "What was I so bummed about anyway?"

Use Your Past to Guide You

When you feel depression creeping back into your life, don't get stuck. Think back on times when you felt bad and how you were able to come out of it.

Don't Let Your Depression Control Your Decision Making

Don't make any big decisions when your mood is at its worst. You may have already learned from experience that if you do this, you will regret it. Learn to tell yourself, "I don't always think the best when I'm like this, so I'd better ride it out before I make any huge decisions."

Let Your Friends Know What's Up

When you are depressed, you aren't always easy to be friends with. You might lose your temper or pull back from your friends. Your friends might be clueless about why you have changed the way you treat them. They might think you are mad at them. If they feel they have done nothing wrong, they may get mad at you. If you just tell them you are sad and that you're not upset with them and don't feel like hanging out, they will probably understand. You need friends. Even though you may not want to spend a lot of time with them now, you will in the future. Don't let your mood ruin your relationships.

Find Something that Soothes Your Soul

It is everyone's responsibility to learn about what kinds of healthy things make them feel better when they are bummed. Only you can do this because every person is different. The list below has some suggestions that other teens have used to make them feel better when they were down.

- Listen to certain music
- Write or read
- Be creative by playing an instrument, painting, taking photos, writing songs, or writing poetry
- Put energy into physical activities such as shooting hoops, hitting a tennis ball, in-line skating, skateboarding, walking, or running
- Get your feelings out by creating a collage or scrapbook, spending time recording songs that express how you feel, or journaling
- Watch your favorite movie and then tell someone why it is your favorite movie
- Pray or meditate
- Do something healthy that makes you feel better but does not cause other problems for you

Avoid Doing Things that Make You Feel Worse

One of the weird things about being depressed it that you often feel drawn into behavior that makes you feel worse. This is an example of allowing your depression to control your behavior. If you want to feel better, you have to recognize what this behavior is and how to avoid it. Things that make depressed adolescents feel worse are listed below.

- Listening to certain music, like music that describes the world as hopeless and awful. A certain amount of this might be okay, but enough is enough.
- Doing any behavior that goes against your value system and makes you feel bad about yourself.
- Dwelling on mistakes and beating yourself up for things that cannot be changed now.
- Cutting yourself off from people who care about you.
- Cutting yourself off from activities that you like.
- Drinking or using drugs.
- Hanging out with people who make you feel worse about yourself.

Avoid People Who Make You Feel Worse

You probably realize that who you hang around with can affect your mood. Some people can always make you laugh, some make you think, and some make you feel worse about yourself and the world. You might feel bad when you are with them because they are critical or negative, tease a lot, or are just mean. These people feed into the kind of thinking you are trying to change. When you are depressed and working to feel better, you may need to avoid certain people.

Find People Who Make You Feel Better

It makes sense that some people are better for your mood than others. When you are working to improve your mood, stay in contact with these people. There is no magic formula to figure out who these people are for you. It may be someone who makes you laugh, will listen to you, or understands what it is like to be depressed because they have learned how to manage their own depression. You know who these people are in your life. Get in contact with them.

Don't Think So Much

When you feel bad, your thoughts might get fixed on obsessing about how bad you feel and trying to figure out why. The more you sit around and focus on how bad you feel, the worse you will feel. When you analyze and obsess on things that are not good, you may overlook the good things and focus on the bad. Do think about your feelings, but focusing too much on them can become overwhelming.

Do Something for Someone Else

Make a contribution. Help a friend with a problem but be careful not to take on the problems of the world. Volunteer at a homeless shelter, a children's hospital, do service work through your church, or work at a camp for kids who don't have much. All these activities will help you change your focus from yourself to others. They will also help expand your outlook and make you feel good about yourself when you realize that you have something to offer others.

Find Someone to "Get Your Back" When it Comes to Your Mood

Friends often help friends by "getting each other's backs." That means, sometimes, someone else can see things that you can't see (like things behind you). This all starts by trusting someone who knows you well and is not afraid to tell you the truth. This person can be a friend, therapist, pastor, parent, relative, or a friend's parent. You need someone who can tell you like it is and will let you know when your perceptions are distorted or out of whack. This person can help you make decisions. Listen to their advice when you are not in a good place to make decisions on your own.

Julie's Thoughts on the Reality of Life

Julie is a bright, perceptive middle school student who struggled with her mood from a very young age. She struggled with trying to be happy even though things were not ever perfect for her. Julie's thoughts are a great example of how she learned to manage her mood by accepting the realities of life.

· JULIE'S STORY ·

Life will never always go your way no matter how much you try or how much effort you put into it. People screw up. Life screws up. There is no way of changing it. People die and people become depressed. People will make your life hell and people will make your life all the better. People will make you sad, mad, hurt, vengeful, and even happier, nicer, and more accepting.

There will be hard, bad, happy, and good times. There will always be negative and positive spots. You will cry and you will hurt. You will make others cry and you will hurt others. Not everyone in the world is nice; not everyone can be how you want them to be. You can't be everything to everyone and everyone can't be everything to you. The people you love may not love you. You may not love the people who love you.

You won't always get your way, but neither will anyone else. You will have secrets of your own and of others. You will always be ashamed of something and proud of something else. You will lose good friends and gain great friends. Memories will last forever and slip away and be lost in time. You will witness some big events and just live to hear about the others. You will wrong someone, and someone will wrong you. You will not always look your best, but neither will you always look your worst. You will see the inside beauty of people and they will see it in you. You will look past people's quirks and they will look past yours. You will judge people, and people will judge you. You may feel alone, but you will never be completely alone.

Life requires things from you, and you require things from life. You have to learn to look past the ugliness and see the beauty. You have to look past the negative and see the positive. You have to look past the frown and see a smile. You have to forgive and hope that you will be forgiven too. You have to stick with it and never give up.

Life can be hard, but it's only as hard as you make it. It's your life, not anyone else's. Figure out what you want from it. Life will never always go your way, but if you look past all the bad, there will always be good. One day can go horribly wrong, but the sun still rises the next day and you must too. Learn to trust and love people and they will come to love and trust you too.

Life is about winning and losing. Losing makes you stronger. Critique yourself, but not too much. Life will never be perfect, so stop trying to make it that way. Just live day by day. Let the past be the past and the future be the future. When something doesn't go your way, learn from it. Don't dwell on it. What's done is done and you will never be able to change it. Make a difference in someone else's life. You have to work to get something you want. If you work hard enough, you will get what you deserve. Never give up. After all, if you want a rainbow, you have to put up with the rain. It's the reality of life.

Activity 11, *Ways to Make Your Mood Better,* will help you discover specific ways to improve your mood.

 **Complete Activity 11**

WAYS TO MAKE YOUR
MOOD BETTER

Name: _____

DIRECTIONS: Read through each suggestion and fill in the blanks as best as you can.

1. Write about a bad time that seemed much worse when you were going through it than when it was over.

   _____

   _____

   _____

   _____

   _____

   _____

2. How long did the situation last?

   _____

3. What good things have happened in your life between then and now?

   _____

   _____

   _____

   _____

   _____

   _____

   _____

Activity 11 continued on next page

4. Give some examples of decisions you made when you were depressed that you later regretted.

_____

_____

_____

_____

_____

5. Which friends do you need to talk to about your depression?

_____

_____

_____

_____

_____

6. What do you need to let them know about your mood?

_____

_____

_____

_____

_____

Activity 11 continued on next page

7. What can your friends do to help you when you are depressed?

   _____

   _____

   _____

   _____

   _____

   _____

8. List three activities you can do that help you feel better.

   a. _____

   _____

   b. _____

   _____

   c. _____

   _____

9. Now list three activities you should avoid.

   a. _____

   _____

   b. _____

   _____

   c. _____

   _____

Activity 11 continued on next page

10. Who are the people you should not be around when you are depressed?

   _____

   _____

   _____

   _____

11. Why should you avoid these people?

   _____

   _____

   _____

   _____

   _____

12. Who are the people you should seek out when you are depressed?

   _____

   _____

   _____

   _____

13. What is it about these people that makes you feel better?

   _____

   _____

   _____

   _____

   _____

Activity 11 continued on next page

14. What are some things that you think about too often?

_____

_____

_____

_____

15. What is something you can do for someone else?

_____

_____

_____

_____

16. Write down the names of people you trust enough to "get your back" when you are not in a good place.

_____

_____

_____

_____

17. What are the things you need from these people to help you when your depression is controlling your decision making?

_____

_____

_____

_____

ALCOHOL AND OTHER DRUGS

ALCOHOL AND OTHER DRUGS

The Top Seven Reasons Teens Don't Want to Give Up Alcohol and Other Drugs

When it comes to hanging onto using alcohol and other drugs, you can come up with all kinds of reasons not to make changes in your use. Let's take a look at some of these—I mean really take a look.

Reason Number 1: "I like it!"

Duh!!! Of course you like it, that's why you do it. That's the only reason anyone ever does it. The truth is that you may like it too much. You may like it so much that you continue to do it even though it is messing things up. You have to ask yourself, "Why do I like it so much?" Maybe it's because you think it helps you deal with your awful mood. Actually, it might be contributing to it. So the question is, "Do you like it enough to continue to feel terrible, just so you can keep doing it?" If so, that's a problem.

Reason Number 2: "It's not a problem, I don't do it that much, I could quit if I really wanted to."

Well that's good news! The time to quit is when you can. It really sucks to try and quit once you have gone so far that you can't quit. So, if you want to feel better, now would be a good time to think about wanting to quit.

Reason Number 3: "I know people who are much worse than I am."

Don't we all. In fact, I know a lot of people who have died. What difference does that make? Do you want to just continue down this road until you are worse off than anyone you know?

Reason Number 4: "I still want to do it!"

I have a friend who quit smoking. He quit after a couple of failed attempts. I asked him how he was finally able to quit. He said, "I always thought that one day I would wake up and want to quit smoking. And I thought the day I wanted to quit would be the day that I would quit. I finally realized that I would always want to smoke no matter what. There would never be a time when I wouldn't still want to smoke. So the time to quit was now." Great point! You will probably always want to get a buzz of some sort. If you are ever going to quit, you are going to have to quit without putting it off—in other words, now.

Reason Number 5: "I'm still young. I will quit when I am older."

Really? When adolescents tell me this, I tell them that I do not want them sitting in my office when they are twenty-one years old telling me that they have to quit using drugs. Why don't I want to have this conversation? Because it's painful. I got a call from someone whom I hadn't seen in a few years asking if she could stop by and see me. When she got to my office, she was a mess. She told me how she really screwed up. She had blown it with her parents, college, and her boyfriend. She was depressed, anxious, and even suicidal. She admitted she was ready to work on her mood and give up drugs and alcohol. Getting clean and sober at this point—with no support, no financial assistance, no place to live—is really hard. While I was proud of her for making this choice, I thought how sad it was that she had to lose so much, waste so much time, and fail so many times before she realized this. Better late than never, but the earlier the better.

Reason Number 6: "But I know a kid who gets high every day and is the valedictorian of his class."

Well, it's a pretty safe bet that you are not the valedictorian of your class, so what does that have to do with anything? A couple years ago, the valedictorian of a local senior class came into treatment with me. Needless to say, I could have done without him looking at me and informing me, "I'm the valedictorian of my senior class and I go to school baked every day. What do you think of that?" The only thing I could think to say was, "I think it's sad that someone as smart as you has to be checked out of your life part of every day."

Reason Number 7: "I'm still having fun doing it."

This may be true, but then again, maybe it's not. Look back on the last drunken high school party you attended. Chances are people were behaving in ways you didn't like. Maybe there was some kid who was drunk, obnoxious, and annoying. Maybe some other guys were trying to pick fights. Let's not forget the people who were so drunk they were throwing up all over the place. Was there someone there who was drunk and crying while they tried to share their very sad life story with anyone who would listen? Maybe there was someone hooking up with someone else's guy or girl. Probably someone was stumbling to their car ready to drive home drunk. Did you spend some time worrying about the cops busting you or your parents finding out what you were doing? Don't forget the terrible mood you found yourself in the next day because you were hungover or worried about what you did while in a blackout. Is this your idea of fun?

Find out how alcohol and other drugs just add to your depression—not help it—in Activity 12, *Alcohol, Drugs, and Depression Don't Mix.*

 **Complete Activity 12**

ALCOHOL, DRUGS, AND DEPRESSION DON'T MIX

Name: _____

DIRECTIONS: Fill in the blanks as best as you can.

Alcohol and Other Drugs

a. What is your favorite reason for not wanting to give up drugs or drinking?

_____

_____

_____

_____

b. What B.S. do you see in this line of reasoning?

_____

_____

_____

_____

Activity 12 continued on next page

What Does It Mean to Have a Drug or Alcohol Problem?

If you have a mood problem, you don't have to be addicted to substances like alcohol or other drugs for them to be a problem for you. Let's just take a look at a few simple guidelines for what defines a "problem" with drugs.

1. **If it causes a problem, then it is a problem.** If something has created problems for you in your life, then it is a problem for you. Maybe you aren't shooting needles into your arm at this point, but does it really have to be that bad before you decide to do something about it?

   a. What specific problems have drugs or alcohol caused for you at home, school, with friends, parents, or teachers?

   _____

   _____

   _____

   _____

   _____

   _____

   _____

   _____

   _____

   _____

   _____

   _____

   _____

   _____

   _____

Activity 12 continued on next page

2. **Anything you try to do less of and end up doing more of is a problem.** How many times have you said, "I can quit," or "I'm going to quit," or "I will cut back"? And as you tried to do that, you found yourself right back where you started or even further back. Doesn't it seem strange that you keep trying to do less and you always end up doing more?

   a. When was the last time you ended up using more or using again after you told yourself you would change your alcohol or other drug use or quit using all together?

   _____

   _____

3. **The more you use, the more you use.** They call this progression. It means that drinking some leads to drinking more often and in larger amounts. For example, smoking pot leads to smoking more pot. No one wakes up one Sunday morning and says, "Oh no! I didn't have a drug problem last night when I went to bed, but this morning I have one." It all happens gradually. Using a small amount progresses to using more and more until one day you realize that you have a drug problem.

   a. At what age did you start drinking alcohol? _____

   Write a brief history of your drinking. Start out with how often and how much you drank in the beginning and how this changed over time.

   _____

   _____

   _____

   _____

   _____

Activity 12 continued on next page

b. At what age did you start using marijuana? _____

Write a brief history of your marijuana use. Start out with how often and how much you smoked in the beginning, how much it took to get you high, and how this has changed over time.

_____

_____

_____

_____

_____

_____

_____

_____

c. Based on your past experiences, what do you think will happen next if you continue to use pot or drink alcohol?

_____

_____

_____

_____

_____

_____

_____

_____

_____

_____

_____

Activity 12 continued on next page

4. **The more you use, the worse things get.** You can blame things on anyone or anything you want, but using alcohol or other drugs causes your problems.

   a. What has gotten worse in your life since you began drinking or using drugs? (For example, friendships, relationships with a boyfriend or girlfriend, family life, grades in school, legal problems, attitude, motivation, self-esteem.)

   _____

   _____

   _____

   _____

5. **It's a problem when you depend on someone to do something for you that you should be able to do for yourself.** If you depend on drugs to have a good time, then drugs are a problem. If you depend on drugs to deal with unpleasant feelings, then drugs are a problem. If you depend on drugs to make you feel comfortable with friends, then drugs are a problem. Why is this a problem? These are all things you need to be able to do on your own without help from drugs.

   a. What should you be able to do yourself that you now depend on drugs to do for you? (For example, getting rid of your stress, getting rid of your nervousness, giving you confidence.)

   _____

   _____

   _____

   _____

   _____

   _____

Quitting Alcohol and Other Drugs

If you don't use, don't start. It is too dangerous and risky for someone who has mood problems. Using will only make a bad situation worse. Using will compound your existing problems so that you have even more problems.

If you do use, stop. Don't cut back or switch drugs. Just stop. For some of you who haven't been using long, quitting may not be too difficult; others may require a great deal of effort.

Just make peace with the fact you can't drink or use drugs now. You don't have to think about forever, just for now.

Activity 13, *What to Do About Alcohol and Other Drugs,* lists some guidelines you can follow to help you stop drinking and using drugs.

 **Complete Activity 13**

WHAT TO DO ABOUT ALCOHOL AND OTHER DRUGS

Name: _____

DIRECTIONS: The guidelines below will help you stop drinking or using other drugs. Read the guidelines and answer the questions as best as you can.

1. **Choose activities that do not center around alcohol and other drug use.** That makes not using or drinking much easier for you. The opportunity to use alcohol or other drugs is all around you. You have probably seen a real difference between activities where alcohol and other drugs may be present and activities that only exist because alcohol and other drugs are there.

    a. What two activities do you need to avoid because they are alcohol- or drug-centered?

    _____

    _____

    _____

    _____

    b. What two activities do you need to focus on that do not center on drinking or using?

    _____

    _____

    _____

    _____

Activity 13 continued on next page

2. Choose to participate in at least some activities in which alcohol and other drugs are not around. The more you see alcohol and other drugs, the more it becomes part of your normal life and the easier it is to make the choice to use.

While you know people use alcohol and other drugs in many social settings, find some places where they don't play any role.

a. What activities can you participate in that never involve alcohol or other drugs?

_____

_____

_____

_____

3. Be accountable. Find someone you know and trust and share with them why it is so important for you not to use or drink. Ask them for help in holding you accountable. It is not their job to stop you, but they can be there to remind you or help you find your way out of tough spots.

a. Who can help you by being an accountability partner?

_____

_____

b. What can you say to this person about your situation?

_____

_____

_____

_____

_____

Activity 13 continued on next page

c. What can this person do to help?

_____

_____

_____

_____

4. **Expand your network of friends.** You do not have to drop your old friends who drink or use drugs; however, there are some things you need to do.

There may be some people you see only because they use or drink. Your entire relationship with them may be based on using. These are people you may need to avoid.

a. Which people do you hang around with only because they drink or use?

_____

_____

_____

5. **There may be some friends who use alcohol and other drugs, but they do not use them heavily or regularly.** You need to ask these friends to call you when they are doing something that does not involve drinking or using so you can get together.

a. Which friends fit into this category?

_____

_____

_____

Activity 13 continued on next page

b. What can you say to these friends?

_____

_____

_____

_____

_____

6. You may need to work to expand your network of friends.
All you have to do is meet one person who does not drink or use. Ask them to introduce you to more people until you have several people in your network of friends who do not drink or use.

a. Who can help you expand your social network?

_____

_____

_____

7. Try to find others who have gone through what you are going through. Sometimes the best support comes from people who have quit using or drinking themselves.

a. Who has been through what you are going through?

_____

_____

_____

Activity 13 continued on next page

8. Always plan an exit route. Sometimes you don't know when you will encounter a drinking or drug-using situation. Always have an exit plan.

a. What are some possible situations that might be difficult for you?

_____

_____

_____

_____

_____

b. What are some possible escape plans for these situations?

_____

_____

_____

_____

_____

9. Seek help if you need it. If you are unable to discontinue your drinking or using, get help. This workbook is not intended to be a substitute for treatment. If you need help, here are some important things to consider:

• Get to a Twelve Step meeting sponsored by Alcoholics Anonymous (AA). This is the most effective way to find a support group and get help with your alcohol or drug problem. Just get to a meeting and AA members will help you with the rest. (You can find a list of local AA chapters in the phonebook.)

• Find a counselor you trust, then trust them with the truth.

• Work with the counselor. If that does not work, have them refer you to a drug-treatment provider.

Activity 13 continued on next page

a. List two things you will do if you are unable to stop your drinking or using.

   1. _____

      _____

      _____

   2. _____

      _____

      _____

MARIJUANA USE

MARIJUANA USE

James was a talented, creative, intelligent, gifted, and likable sixteen-year-old. He was also addicted to marijuana and severely depressed. During his recovery, he wrote about his relationship with his drug of choice—pot.

• JAMES'S STORY •

Once upon a teenage dream there was this glamorous box, or so it seemed. The flashy box held smiles, laughter, and an extraordinary euphoria that no one could touch. It was spectacular. A glimmer shined from it, catching my eye from an incredible distance and drawing me closer and closer. Everything and anything that I could possibly imagine came with the box of a teenage dream. It gave me fame, glory, insight, and outrageous feelings that tingled every extreme of my body. My mind filled with excitement of new words and ecstatic states. Day by day in this box a teenage dream grew, lighting the way into the greatest fantasy of all in reality.

Over time, this box and I became one. It captivated me, wrapping itself around me like a warm blanket on a cold, snowy winter day. I was intertwined with the whole majestical euphoria of this box. We grew and grew with each great experience, building strength together.

But for some odd reason the box was losing some of its glimmer, some of its spectacular image. The brilliant walls of the box were slowly being replaced by stone. The laughs, smiles, fame, and glory all started to dwindle away, causing some dismay. It became a necessity to be within the box of a teenage dream. This grand box had consumed me, shackling me to the center of this now dungeon scene. The glimmer now left like the sunset and the sky filled with an overwhelming darkness. The stone walls that I built were all very hard, cold, and damp. I curled into a ball in the corner of the box of a teenage dream, crying and shaking with fear.

The only thing that remained from the fabulous box was one glimmer of light that peeked through a crack and stared me in the eyes. This glimmering light tortured my very being, mocking the days that had come and gone. I clawed and dug, trying to close the crack, but it was not possible. My fingers bled and tears filled my eyes as I thought about what I had constructed. My soul slowly disappeared with every teardrop that fell. My once beautiful box had turned on me, consuming me like a wild pack of dogs feeding on the last morsel of food. Now all that remained was the glory of darkness and fear. I was trapped in the agony of depression.

We can all hit rock bottom with nowhere to run or hide at some point in our lives. I know. I have been there. I created my fabulous fantasy box. We all try to find this fantasy land where everything is absolutely perfect and nothing can affect us, but what we need to understand is that there are no guarantees. The only guarantee is where there is a light, there is hope. We need to try to reach the light, instead of trying to cover it up. Where there is hope, there is an out. I know, because I found mine.

A Word About Weed

James's writing shows the true nature of marijuana and adolescence. It is charming, seductive, fun, and intriguing and offers many promises of making things better. Eventually, the pot sneaks into your life, creates problems you never saw coming, and takes away hope and happiness. James found a way beyond this. The first step in this journey was to get completely honest with himself about what it was really like living life as a "pot head."

Many teens know they need to stay away from or give up their "serious" drugs. However, most teens (and many adults as well) underestimate the power of marijuana, especially for someone who is depressed. Since teens with depression often use pot, it's important to say a few words about this drug. Activity 14, *What's the Deal with Pot?,* sums up a few words about this drug.

 **Complete Activity 14**

WHAT'S THE DEAL WITH POT?

Name: _____

DIRECTIONS: Read through each "word" on marijuana and answer the questions as best as you can.

Word #1

Marijuana is a sneaky drug. It slowly creeps up on you a little bit at a time. Other drugs are not quite so sneaky. If you crawl around on the floor of a crack house looking for a rock to smoke, something inside you calls out, "This is pitiful; I'm such an addict." Drugs like cocaine, heroin, ecstasy, and pills can have a big impact on your life in a short period of time. It's hard to deny an addiction to them once you become addicted.

Pot gradually creeps into your life, altering your mood and personality a little bit at a time. It is so gradual that you don't even recognize the change until one day you wake up, look in the mirror, and say, "Dude, how did this happen to me? I can't believe how much I am getting high." The problem is, that by the time you recognize that it is a problem, you probably won't care that it is. One of the main problems with pot is that it makes you not care. It takes over your life, inch by inch, and robs you of your motivation to do anything about it.

a. Think back on your pot use history. How has that use changed since you began using?

_____

_____

_____

_____

_____

Activity 14 continued on next page

Word #2

Yes, marijuana is natural, and it is a plant, herb, or whatever else you want to call it. Opium, cocaine, and poison sumac are also plants. That doesn't mean it's a good idea to put them in your body. It doesn't make it any safer. The fact that marijuana is a plant doesn't mean it doesn't mess with your mood.

Word #3

People say pot is not physically addicting. If that's true, then why is it so hard to give up? People try, intend, and promise to give it up but keep right on doing it. With pot, you get addicted to the high. That is what keeps you coming back.

a. Have you ever tried to change how much or how often you smoke pot?

       ○ Yes   ○ No

b. What did you notice when you tried to cut back or quit? Did you miss it?

_____

_____

c. Was quitting harder than you expected it to be? Explain.

_____

_____

d. Were you cranky or irritable? Explain.

_____

_____

Activity 14 continued on next page

Word #4

Marijuana is a gateway drug, and it is a bad gateway. I keep hearing that the problem with marijuana is that it could and often does lead to the use of other drugs. The problem with pot is that it leads to more pot use. Even if you've never used other drugs, smoking pot can be a problem when it messes up your mood. Lying to friends and family, changing your attitude about school, getting in trouble with the law, and making you not give a crap about life becomes a way of life for you. And that's a problem. So think of it this way: If marijuana is a gateway drug, a lot of people are stuck in the gateway and that's a problem in and of itself.

a. What kinds of problems do you have because of your marijuana use?

_____

_____

_____

_____

_____

Word #5

Some people say marijuana is not any worse than alcohol. They say it should be legal like alcohol. It's true that it is legal for adults to drink alcohol. But that doesn't mean that it is not a problem for adults, even if they drink legally. Alcoholism is a huge problem for many adults. Look at it this way: If it screws up your life, what difference does it make if it is legal or illegal?

Pot and Growing Up

Let's face it. It takes a lot of work to go from being a child to being an adult. That process is called adolescence. It lasts for several years because a lot has to be done in that time. In the world of cell phones, instant messages, microwaves, and fast food, we have come to expect things to be quick and easy. Adolescence is not quick and easy. It's long and difficult, especially if you are struggling with a mood disorder. People (adults included) do not always have the patience for adolescence to be completed and adulthood to start. Everyone looks for a quick, easy solution to this phase of life.

Some young people feel like marijuana makes adolescence easier. It creates the illusion that you are soaring through your teenage years with little effort. That's one reason some people are so attracted to it. Unfortunately, marijuana makes you feel like you're mastering the challenges of adolescence when, in fact, it's preventing you from doing what you need to do.

Activity 15, *Weed: A Lazy Teen Solution to Adolescence,* takes a look at the tasks you need to accomplish during adolescence and how pot interferes with completing those tasks.

 **Complete Activity 15**

WEED: A LAZY TEEN SOLUTION TO ADOLESCENCE

Name: _____

DIRECTIONS: Below is a list of tasks you need to accomplish during adolescence and ways drug use interferes with those tasks. Read through each task and fill in the blanks as best as you can.

TASK NUMBER ONE: Learn to Deal with Feelings

Once a young person moves into adolescence, he or she experiences intense new emotions that are not always easy to deal with. Both the good feelings and unpleasant feelings are intense. We learn to deal with these feelings by experiencing them fully and learning from them. As we mature, we become familiar with feelings. We know how to experience them without becoming overwhelmed. It's an important part of growing up.

By using drugs, we separate ourselves from our feelings. Marijuana does not make anyone not feel; it just makes you care less about the feelings you have. It becomes easy to "get high" instead of expressing feelings. The funny thing is that it tricks you into thinking you are dealing with your feelings, when you are just separating yourself from them. In other words, it's a lazy way to survive feelings that need to be experienced.

a. How are you dealing with your feelings, particularly the difficult ones?

_____

_____

_____

_____

_____

_____

Activity 15 continued on next page

b. Write down two examples of how your drug or alcohol use has interfered with your ability to deal with your feelings.

1. _____

   _____

   _____

2. _____

   _____

   _____

TASK NUMBER TWO: Learn to Think Awesome Thoughts

One of the greatest things that happens when puberty kicks in is that hormones released in the brain allow us to think in different ways. In other words, the brain kicks into high gear and thinks of ideas and concepts that are incredible and impressive. It's great to have awesome thoughts. It's also great to connect with other people who have awesome thoughts and sit around and share these thoughts. The adult part of the brain allows us to put those thoughts into action.

One of the intriguing things about smoking pot is that everyone sits around and shares all their drug-induced insights about the world. The problem is, you are perfectly capable of having these thoughts when you are not high. In fact, you need to be working on developing your brain. When all your great thoughts are drug-induced, they are not your own. Marijuana use at an early age actually prevents your brain from developing the ability to think abstractly, and abstract thinking is where awesome thoughts come from.

a. What have you learned here about your developing brain?

   _____

   _____

   _____

Activity 15 continued on next page

_____

_____

_____

b. Write down a time when you felt that other people could remember better or understand things easier than you.

_____

_____

_____

c. Brain development tends to stop at whatever age you began using regularly. If you are a regular user or drinker, what age were you when you started using regularly?

_____

TASK NUMBER THREE: Learn to Entertain Yourself

We clinical types like to call this task "leisure skills." When you are a little kid, other people knock themselves out trying to entertain you. Adults take kids everywhere, plan parties and play groups, and center vacations and holidays around what will be fun for the kids. Trust me. Someone probably put a great deal of effort into making sure you were having a good time when you were a small child.

Once you reach adolescence, people stop planning your entertainment. You are left to learn the important adult tasks of learning to have fun on your own. It might take some effort to have a good time, and it certainly should be worth the effort.

When you drink, smoke weed, or use other drugs, you get lazy about entertaining yourself. I don't know how many times I hear kids tell me, "We party because there is nothing else to do." My response is always the same, "Yes there is; you're just too lazy to put effort into having a good time."

Activity 15 continued on next page

When you are smoking weed, you sit around watching stupid movies, laughing at stupid things that are not that funny. You think you are having a good time. The idea of not smoking weed seems boring, but let's face it, how much fun will you really be missing?

Drug use makes you think you are learning to entertain yourself and have a good time. The truth is that you are depending on your drug use to do this for you.

a. What do you do (other than using or drinking) to entertain yourself?

_____

_____

_____

b. When have you relied on drugs and alcohol to entertain yourself?

_____

_____

_____

c. What two things do you do to entertain yourself that does not include drinking or drug use?

1. _____

_____

_____

2. _____

_____

_____

Activity 15 continued on next page

TASK NUMBER FOUR: Develop Social Confidence

Remember when you first entered middle school or junior high? Suddenly, you became painfully aware of other people. You became aware of who did and didn't like you, who was popular and why. While trying to figure out all this complicated stuff, some people become self-conscious and uncomfortable being in this new environment. People start to worry about looking or sounding stupid. They might be afraid to go into a new situation because they are concerned no one will like them or they won't know how to act.

Middle school and high school is a time for people to face those awkward and sometimes painful social situations. It's a time to discover that they can talk to people they do not know and make new friends. People often discover something interesting during this time—that if they drink or use drugs, they do not feel quite so uncomfortable and awkward. Instead of living through those unpleasant feelings and learning how to get past them, people depend on their alcohol and other drugs to do this for them. As a result, other people their age develop social confidence and the drug-using teens get left behind.

a. List examples of how you have used alcohol or other drugs to help you overcome social awkwardness.

    _____

    _____

    _____

b. How do you feel when you are with a group of people who you do not know very well?

    _____

    _____

    _____

Activity 15 continued on next page

c. Make a commitment to practice developing social confidence. What social situations are you willing to face without using alcohol or other drugs?

_____

_____

_____

_____

_____

TASK NUMBER FIVE: Learn to Develop Real Relationships

Developing real relationships means learning how to look people in the eye and tell them what you really think, dream, hope, and believe. Let them see the real you. Find people who can give you honest feedback. These are people who can get mad at you, see your ugly side, and still love you when it is all said and done. These types of relationships won't be found when drug use and drinking are the focus of the relationships. It does not count if you can only share these parts of yourself when you are high or drunk with other people who are high or drunk. The drug- and alcohol-induced "deep" conversations make people think they are forming these real relationships, but they are not. What you learn from real relationships will shape your relationships for the rest of your life. It's something you have to do yourself, without drugs or alcohol. Weed makes you think you are doing what you need to do to grow up; but in fact, you are just pretending to grow up.

a. Give two examples of how you have used drugs and alcohol to build relationships.

1. _____

   _____

   _____

Activity 15 continued on next page

_____

_____

_____

_____

2. _____

_____

_____

_____

_____

_____

Hazelden Publishing and Educational Services is a division of the Hazelden Foundation, a not-for-profit organization. Since 1949, Hazelden has been a leader in promoting the dignity and treatment of people afflicted with the disease of chemical dependency.

The mission of the foundation is to improve the quality of life for individuals, families, and communities by providing a national continuum of information, education, and recovery services that are widely accessible; to advance the field through research and training; and to improve our quality and effectiveness through continuous improvement and innovation.

Stemming from that, the mission of this division is to provide quality information and support to people wherever they may be in their personal journey—from education and early intervention, through treatment and recovery, to personal and spiritual growth.

Although our treatment programs do not necessarily use everything Hazelden publishes, our bibliotherapeutic materials support our mission and the Twelve Step philosophy upon which it is based. We encourage your comments and feedback.

The headquarters of the Hazelden Foundation are in Center City, Minnesota. Additional treatment facilities are located in Chicago, Illinois; Newberg, Oregon; New York, New York; Plymouth, Minnesota; St. Paul, Minnesota; and West Palm Beach, Florida. At these sites, we provide a continuum of care for men and women of all ages. Our Plymouth facility is designed specifically for youth and families.

For more information on Hazelden,
please call **1-800-257-7800.**

Or you may access our World Wide Web site
on the Internet at **www.hazelden.org.**